To: M

Love:

2016

CAT SELFIES

CHARLIE ELLIS

SUMMERSDALE PUBLISHERS LTD
46 WEST STREET
CHICHESTER
WEST SUSSEX
PO19 1RP
UK

WWW.SUMMERSDALE.COM

PRINTED AND BOUND IN THE CZECH REPUBLIC

ISBN: 978-1-84953-646-2

SUBSTANTIAL DISCOUNTS ON BULK QUANTITIES OF SUMMERSDALE BOOKS ARE AVAILABLE TO CORPORATIONS, PROFESSIONAL ASSOCIATIONS AND OTHER ORGANISATIONS. FOR DETAILS CONTACT NICKY DOUGLAS BY TELEPHONE: +44 (0) 1243 756902, FAX: +44 (0) 1243 786300 OR EMAIL: NICKY@SUMMERSDALE.COM.

TO...

FROM...

#SHOWYOURBESTANGLE

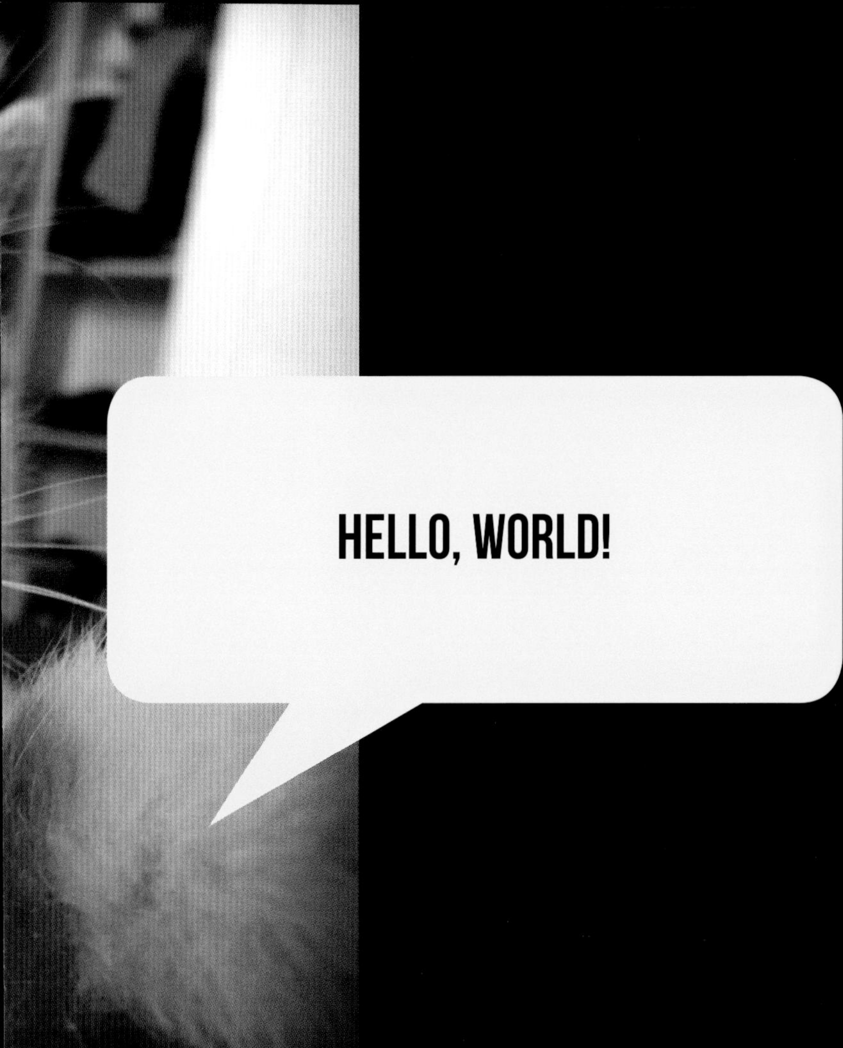
HELLO, WORLD!

#VAMPIRECAT

#TWILIGHT

I SAY, A SPOT OF DINNER WOULDN'T GO AMISS, WOT WOT!

#EXISTENTIALANGUISH

WELCOME TO DAY 2 OF OPERATION KILL NEXT DOOR'S GERBIL. FOLLOW MY PROGRESS ON #DIENIBBLESDIE

NAME:
AGE:
TITLE:
DISLIKES:

ELGAR
2 YEARS
KING OF HIS PINK CUBE
FAKE OWLS

#ARTYSELFIE

WATCHING HORROR FILMS ALONE AT NIGHT — THAT'S JUST HOW TOUGH I AM.

#TOOMUCHCATNIP

#PRIMALSCREAM

NAME:	WALTER
AGE:	8 YEARS
SPEED:	LIKE A SQUIRREL IN FLIGHT
FEARS:	TORTOISES
BACKSIDE:	OFTEN WET FROM OVERZEALOUS POND-DIPPING

#COOLFORCATS

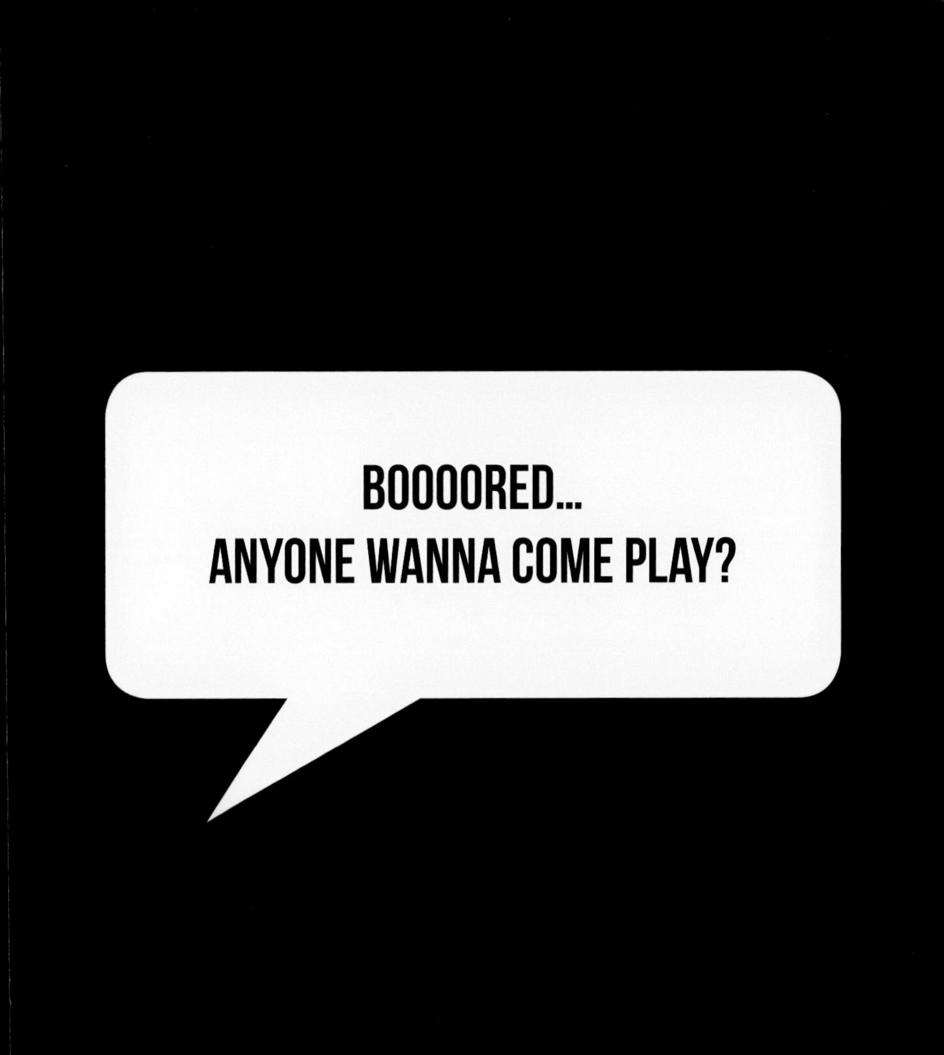
BOOOORED...
ANYONE WANNA COME PLAY?

#SMOULDERRRRRRR

MAN, I HAVE GOT TO EVEN OUT MY TAN LINES.

NICKNAME:	MAXOU
FAVOURITE MODE OF TRANSPORT:	RIDING IN A MOTORCYCLE SADDLEBAG
MORTAL ENEMY:	CARNIVOROUS PLANTS

#MEANCATS

THIS PEBBLE-DASH IS SURPRISINGLY COMFORTABLE.

#EXTREMESELFIE

#JAZZHAND

WHY HAVEN'T THEY MADE
KEYPADS THAT ARE BIG
ENOUGH FOR PAWS YET?

NICKNAME: SADFACE

AGE: 7 YEARS

LIKES: EATING GRASS, FURRY FEMALE CATS, SMELLING SHOES

DISLIKES: NOT EATING GRASS, INSERTING HEAD INTO DARK HOLES, RUNNING MEN

#BLAIRCATPROJECT

NAME:  POLO

LIKES: BEING THE FANCIEST CAT IN TOWN

DISLIKES: HAVING A WHISKER OUT OF PLACE

#STRETCHSELFIE

YEAH, I'M JUST NATURALLY THIS SOFT AND FLUFFY.

#IKNOWRIGHT

NAME: ROXAS

SPECIAL SKILL: EXPERT FREE-RUNNER

PREFERRED SLEEPING PLACE: INSIDE A JACKET

#WHATDIDIDOLASTNIGHT?

CURIOSITY DID *WHAT* TO THE CAT?

#SNOWDAY

NAME: KITTY

FREQUENTLY FOUND: LOUNGING ON THE SOFA

LIKES: EVERYONE ELSE'S FOOD

NAME: 貓仔 (CAT IN CHINESE)

SPECIAL SKILL: CAN TRACK DOWN HIS FAVOURITE SNACK AT 10,000 PACES

HOBBIES: PLAYING WITH HIS OWN TAIL

#SITTINGPRETTY

#CATNAP

HAVE YOU EVER BEEN SO COMFORTABLE YOU'VE STARTED TO MELT INTO YOUR SOFA?

NAME: SWEEP

LIKES: SHOWING PEOPLE HIS BELLY

DISLIKES: PEOPLE TOUCHING HIS BELLY

EXTREME DISLIKES: HIS BROTHER GETTING MORE
ATTENTION THAN HIM

#CHILLINGINMYLAIR

#EVILGENIUS

GOODNIGHT, CATBOOKERS.
I'M OFF TO BED.

#SELFIEADDICTS

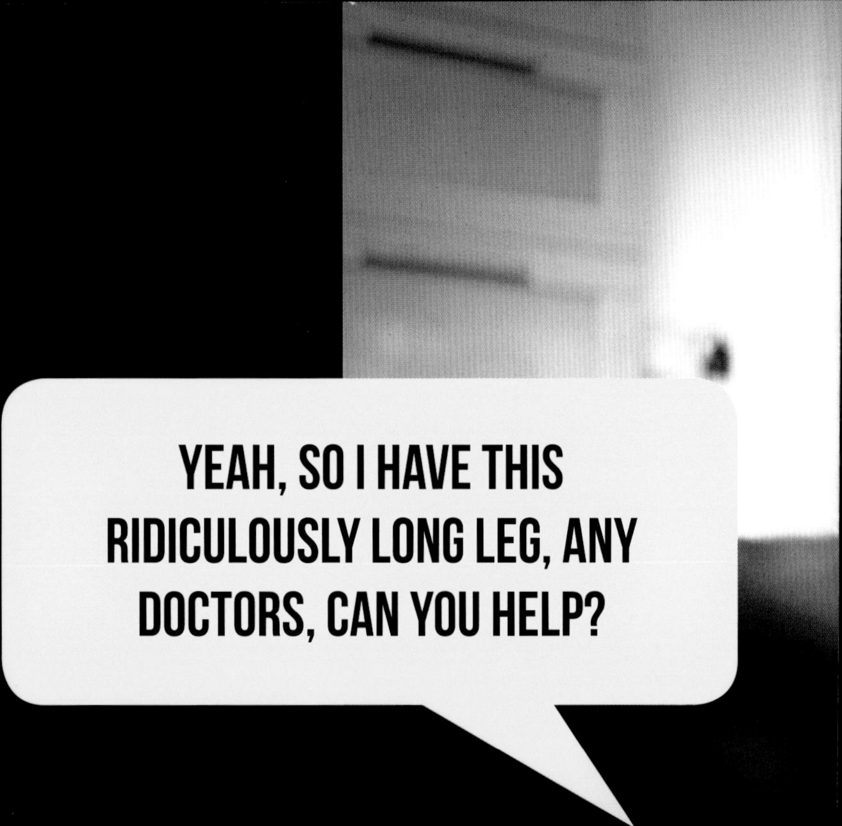
YEAH, SO I HAVE THIS RIDICULOUSLY LONG LEG, ANY DOCTORS, CAN YOU HELP?

NAME: BAILEY

LIKES: BEING THE (VERY NOISY) CENTRE OF ATTENTION

DISLIKES: BEING INTERRUPTED

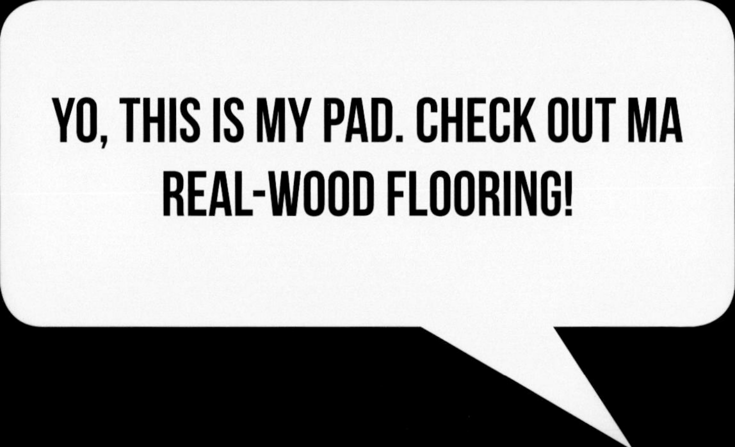
YO, THIS IS MY PAD. CHECK OUT MA REAL-WOOD FLOORING!

#STUBBEDMYTOE

PHOTO CREDITS

DOG SELFIES

CHARLIE ELLIS

DOG SELFIES

ISBN: 978 1 84953 645 5   HARDBACK   £6.99

EVERYONE IS SNAPPING SELFIES AND DOGS ARE NO EXCEPTION! FROM THE SUBLIME TO THE RIDICULOUS, THIS BOOK COLLECTS THE BEST PHOTOS OF MUTTS WHO HAVE TAKEN THE SELFIE CRAZE INTO THEIR OWN PAWS.

IF YOU'RE INTERESTED IN FINDING OUT MORE ABOUT OUR BOOKS,
FIND US ON FACEBOOK AT SUMMERSDALE PUBLISHERS
AND FOLLOW US ON TWITTER AT @SUMMERSDALE.

WWW.SUMMERSDALE.COM